Welcome, Procrastinator!

Do you look at punctual, productive people and wonder what bizarre syndrome drives such behavior? Do you worry that you might start thinking and acting like that too? (Theoretically, of course—worrying is way too exhausting.) If you are among the initiated who know the value of time wasted, join us. *Do It Later!* is designed for the way we time-challenged people work. We're procrastinators— we get the important stuff done . . . when we get around to it. To be productive and creative, we first need to engage in time-sucking activities, such as checking and rechecking our email and social media, organizing our pens, selecting energizing tunes, and getting a third cup of coffee. If you specialize in such delay tactics, or know someone who does, take a leisurely browse through the tips, activities, and wisdom sprinkled throughout this planner—for instance: "Don't sweat the small stuff—just don't do any of it."

Then, start by writing a to-do item in a section that makes sense, such as "Things I have to do but that can wait a day, or two, or three . . ."; or "Small things I have to do before I can do the big things I have to do"; or "Things I absolutely have to do unless I absolutely don't want to do them." *Do It Later!* is also filled with helpful lists, such as "Ways to Instantly De-stress" and "Baby Steps toward Being More Productive." There's even a place to keep track of due dates and grace periods for your bills, a space to plan those crucial tax extensions, room to list contact information for procrastination partners, and weekly doodle blocks for that most beloved procrastination pastime.

Carry your new planner with pride. And if you never get around to starting the tasks you put in it—or even reading past this page—there's always tomorrow, or the day after, or . . .

—Mark Asher, fellow procrastinator

Procrastinator Tip

If done correctly, procrastination is the best antidepressant known to humankind.

Things I have to do but that can wait a day, or two, or three . . .

Small things I have to do before I can do the big things I have to do

Things I absolutely have to do unless I absolutely don't want to do them

Things people have been bugging me to do for a really long time

doodle
block

December 2018

monday

24 358

CHRISTMAS   *tuesday*

25 359

BOXING DAY (CANADA, UK)   *wednesday*
KWANZAA BEGINS

26 360

thursday

27 361

friday

28 362

saturday

◑ **29** 363

december

s	m	t	w	t	f	s
						1
2	3	4	5	6	7	8
9	10	11	12	13	14	15
16	17	18	19	20	21	22
23	24	25	26	27	28	29
30	31					

sunday

30 364

Procrastinator Wisdom

If the devil is in the details, why would anyone want to be detailed?

Things I have to do but that can wait a day, or two, or three . . .

Small things I have to do before I can do the big things I have to do

Things I absolutely have to do unless I absolutely don't want to do them

Things people have been bugging me to do for a really long time

Dec 2018 / Jan 2019

monday

31 ₃₆₅

NEW YEAR'S DAY

tuesday

1 ₁

BANK HOLIDAY (SCOTLAND)

wednesday

2 ₂

---

thursday

3 ₃

---

friday

4 ₄

---

saturday

5 ₅

---

sunday

● **6** ₆

january

s	m	t	w	t	f	s
		1	2	3	4	5
6	7	8	9	10	11	12
13	14	15	16	17	18	19
20	21	22	23	24	25	26
27	28	29	30	31		

Procrastinator Activity

 The only way to handle an extreme weather system is to shut down your work and safely watch it pass.

Things I have to do but that can wait a day, or two, or three . . .

Small things I have to do before I can do the big things I have to do

Things I absolutely have to do unless I absolutely don't want to do them

Things people have been bugging me to do for a really long time

doodle
block

January

monday

7 ₇

tuesday

8 ₈

wednesday

9 ₉

thursday

10 ₁₀

friday

11 ₁₁

saturday

12 ₁₂

sunday

13 ₁₃

january

s	m	t	w	t	f	s
			1	2	3	4	5
6	7	8	9	10	11	12
13	14	15	16	17	18	19
20	21	22	23	24	25	26
27	28	29	30	31		

Procrastinator Tip

Work is like every bad habit—the second you break it you wonder why you didn't do it sooner.

Things I have to do but that can wait a day, or two, or three . . .

Small things I have to do before I can do the big things I have to do

Things I absolutely have to do unless I absolutely don't want to do them

Things people have been bugging me to do for a really long time

doodle
block

January

monday

◗ 14 14

tuesday

15 15

wednesday

16 16

thursday

17 17

friday

18 18

saturday

19 19

sunday

20 20

january

s	m	t	w	t	f	s
		1	2	3	4	5
6	7	8	9	10	11	12
13	14	15	16	17	18	19
20	21	22	23	24	25	26
27	28	29	30	31		

Procrastinator Wisdom

Everyone says, "Don't wait until the last minute." Why are they so hell-bent on taking away my most productive time?

Things I have to do but that can wait a day, or two, or three . . .

Small things I have to do before I can do the big things I have to do

Things I absolutely have to do unless I absolutely don't want to do them

Things people have been bugging me to do for a really long time

doodle block

January

MARTIN LUTHER KING JR. DAY

monday

○ 21 21

tuesday

22 22

wednesday

23 23

thursday

24 24

friday

25 25

saturday

26 26

sunday

◑ 27 27

january

s	m	t	w	t	f	s
			1	2	3	4	5
6	7	8	9	10	11	12
13	14	15	16	17	18	19
20	21	22	23	24	25	26
27	28	29	30	31		

Baby Steps toward Being More Productive

1. Download three productivity apps and read the instructions for all of them.

2. Design a series of productivity posters and then go shopping for suitable frames.

3. Perform a dry run of working harder—without actually doing more work—to simulate how it would feel.

4. Build confidence by treating the smallest of achievements as if you just cured cancer.

5. Sit beside your most productive coworkers and watch them work for a week.

6. Clean the pet hairs, nose hairs, dust clusters, and food crumbs from your keyboard so it's prepared for heavier use.

7. Have a work coach come to your office to make sure nothing is preventing you from being productive.

8. Create a detailed list of the contents of every storage box at your office and home, so anything you need is at your fingertips.

9. Go to the bookstore and read the back flaps of the best-selling business books.

10. Plan a dream two-week vacation so you have a reward in place for when your increased productivity pays off.

Research and list the top 10 most bizarre or interesting customs from various cultures.

1. _____

2. _____

3. _____

4. _____

5. _____

6. _____

7. _____

8. _____

9. _____

10. _____

Procrastinator Tip

Procrastination is a disease of pleasure; overwork is a disease of stress. Pick your poison.

Things I have to do but that can wait a day, or two, or three . . .

Small things I have to do before I can do the big things I have to do

Things I absolutely have to do unless I absolutely don't want to do them

Things people have been bugging me to do for a really long time

doodle
block

Jan / Feb

monday

28 ₂₈

tuesday

29 ₂₉

wednesday

30 ₃₀

thursday

31 ₃₁

friday

1 ₃₂

saturday

2 ₃₃

sunday

3 ₃₄

february

s	m	t	w	t	f	s
					1	2
3	4	5	6	7	8	9
10	11	12	13	14	15	16
17	18	19	20	21	22	23
24	25	26	27	28		

Procrastinator Activity

When you come to a fork in the road, pull over, tie a hammock to two trees, and ponder your choices.

Things I have to do but that can wait a day, or two, or three . . .

Small things I have to do before I can do the big things I have to do

Things I absolutely have to do unless I absolutely don't want to do them

Things people have been bugging me to do for a really long time

doodle block

February

monday

● **4** 35

LUNAR NEW YEAR
tuesday

5 36

wednesday

6 37

thursday

7 38

friday

8 39

saturday

9 40

sunday

10 41

february

s	m	t	w	t	f	s
					1	2
3	4	5	6	7	8	9
10	11	12	13	14	15	16
17	18	19	20	21	22	23
24	25	26	27	28		

Procrastinator Tip

 Time management is nothing more than a system invented by a businessman while procrastinating. Don't trust it.

Things I have to do but that can wait a day, or two, or three . . .

Small things I have to do before I can do the big things I have to do

Things I absolutely have to do unless I absolutely don't want to do them

Things people have been bugging me to do for a really long time

doodle
block

February

monday

11 42

tuesday

◑ **12** 43

wednesday

13 44

VALENTINE'S DAY   thursday

14 45

friday

15 46

saturday

16 47

sunday

17 48

february

s	m	t	w	t	f	s
					1	2
3	4	5	6	7	8	9
10	11	12	13	14	15	16
17	18	19	20	21	22	23
24	25	26	27	28		

Procrastinator Wisdom

They say procrastination is an ailment. I wish my other ailments were so painless!

Things I have to do but that can wait a day, or two, or three . . .

Small things I have to do before I can do the big things I have to do

Things I absolutely have to do unless I absolutely don't want to do them

Things people have been bugging me to do for a really long time

doodle
block

February

PRESENTS' DAY
FAMILY DAY (CANADA, SOME PROVINCES)

monday

18 49

tuesday

○ 19 50

wednesday

20 51

thursday

21 52

friday

22 53

saturday

23 54

sunday

24 55

february

s	m	t	w	t	f	s
					1	2
3	4	5	6	7	8	9
10	11	12	13	14	15	16
17	18	19	20	21	22	23
24	25	26	27	28		

I don't always have the answers, but I always have questions, and they need pondering!

1. Do male ladybugs have masculinity issues?

2. How is it possible that bowhead whales can live for two hundred years?

3. Why do smoke-alarm batteries always seem to die and start beeping in the middle of the night?

4. Why do people have middle names?

5. Why do jobs that impact society the most pay the least?

6. Why are pizzas made as circles?

7. How do we know for certain that there are no two snowflakes exactly alike?

8. Why don't we sneeze in our sleep?

Come up with 10 changes you would implement at your workplace to reduce burnout.

1. _____

2. _____

3. _____

4. _____

5. _____

6. _____

7. _____

8. _____

9. _____

10. _____

Procrastinator Tip

Coffee is not a stimulant to increase your workload; it's a stimulant to chat more, lounge longer, and eat yummy sweets.

Things I have to do but that can wait a day, or two, or three . . .

Small things I have to do before I can do the big things I have to do

Things I absolutely have to do unless I absolutely don't want to do them

Things people have been bugging me to do for a really long time

doodle block

monday

25 56

tuesday

◑ **26** 57

wednesday

27 58

thursday

28 59

ST. DAVID'S DAY (WALES)   *friday*

1 60

saturday

2 61

sunday

3 62

march

s	m	t	w	t	f	s
					1	2
3	4	5	6	7	8	9
10	11	12	13	14	15	16
17	18	19	20	21	22	23
24	25	26	27	28	29	30
31						

Procrastinator Activity

 I read an article online that said to follow your bliss. So I got up from my desk and went straight to my garden.

Things I have to do but that can wait a day, or two, or three . . .

Small things I have to do before I can do the big things I have to do

Things I absolutely have to do unless I absolutely don't want to do them

Things people have been bugging me to do for a really long time

doodle block

March

---

monday

4 63

MARDI GRAS   *tuesday*

5 64

ASH WEDNESDAY   *wednesday*

● **6** 65

---

thursday

7 66

INTERNATIONAL WOMEN'S DAY   *friday*

8 67

---

saturday

9 68

DAYLIGHT SAVING TIME BEGINS   *sunday*

10 69

march

s	m	t	w	t	f	s
					1	2
3	4	5	6	7	8	9
10	11	12	13	14	15	16
17	18	19	20	21	22	23
24	25	26	27	28	29	30
31						

Procrastinator Tip

 I can work at many different speeds, but idle is my favorite gear.

Things I have to do but that can wait a day, or two, or three . . .

Small things I have to do before I can do the big things I have to do

Things I absolutely have to do unless I absolutely don't want to do them

Things people have been bugging me to do for a really long time

doodle
block

monday

11 70

tuesday

12 71

wednesday

13 72

thursday

◐ **14** 73

friday

15 74

saturday

16 75

march						
s	*m*	*t*	*w*	*t*	*f*	*s*
					1	2
3	4	5	6	7	8	9
10	11	12	13	14	15	16
17	18	19	20	21	22	23
24	25	26	27	28	29	30
31						

ST. PATRICK'S DAY

sunday

17 76

Procrastinator Wisdom

Procrastination is a peaceful protest against irrational deadlines.

Things I have to do but that can wait a day, or two, or three . . .

Small things I have to do before I can do the big things I have to do

Things I absolutely have to do unless I absolutely don't want to do them

Things people have been bugging me to do for a really long time

doodle block

March

BANK HOLIDAY (N. IRELAND)

monday

18 77

tuesday

19 78

VERNAL EQUINOX 21:58 UTC

wednesday

20 79

HOLI
PURIM

thursday

○ **21** 80

friday

22 81

saturday

23 82

sunday

24 83

march

s	m	t	w	t	f	s
					1	2
3	4	5	6	7	8	9
10	11	12	13	14	15	16
17	18	19	20	21	22	23
24	25	26	27	28	29	30
31						

Procrastinator Tip

Once you get the hang of it, doing nothing is quite intoxicating.

Things I have to do but that can wait a day, or two, or three . . .

Small things I have to do before I can do the big things I have to do

Things I absolutely have to do unless I absolutely don't want to do them

Things people have been bugging me to do for a really long time

doodle
block

March

monday

25 84

tuesday

26 85

wednesday

27 86

thursday

◑ **28** 87

friday

29 88

saturday

30 89

march

s	m	t	w	t	f	s
					1	2
3	4	5	6	7	8	9
10	11	12	13	14	15	16
17	18	19	20	21	22	23
24	25	26	27	28	29	30
31						

MOTHERING SUNDAY (UK)

SUMMER TIME BEGINS (UK)

sunday

31 90

What to Do When a Severe Case of Limbo Strikes You

1. Do the limbo.

2. Make a list of songs that lament the state of limbo. Start with "Should I Stay or Should I Go?"

3. Confess to your boss that you are prone to limbotic episodes and pressure will only make matters worse.

4. Immediately turn all of your work over to the nearest coworker in the event that your limbo turns into a serious case of procrastination.

5. Destroy your to-do list and start over with one simple task, like taking a nap or emptying the wastebasket.

6. Make a door hanger that says "In Limbo—Privacy Requested."

7. Jump-start your brain by coming up with as many words as you can that rhyme with limbo.

8. Do yoga in your office so you can be more limber when you do the limbo.

List 10 conversation openers that would make you the life of the party.

1. _____

2. _____

3. _____

4. _____

5. _____

6. _____

7. _____

8. _____

9. _____

10. _____

Procrastinator Activity

The best way to appreciate the passage of time is to idly watch it pass.

Things I have to do but that can wait a day, or two, or three . . .

Small things I have to do before I can do the big things I have to do

Things I absolutely have to do unless I absolutely don't want to do them

Things people have been bugging me to do for a really long time

doodle
block

April

monday

1 91

tuesday

2 92

wednesday

3 93

thursday

4 94

friday

● **5** 95

saturday

6 96

sunday

7 97

Procrastinator Wisdom

My doctor has informed me that I'm severely allergic to stressful deadlines and unreasonable bosses. Unfortunately no antibiotic exists.

Things I have to do but that can wait a day, or two, or three . . .

Small things I have to do before I can do the big things I have to do

Things I absolutely have to do unless I absolutely don't want to do them

Things people have been bugging me to do for a really long time

doodle
block

April

monday

8 98

tuesday

9 99

wednesday

10 100

thursday

11 101

friday

◐ **12** 102

saturday

13 103

PALM SUNDAY

sunday

14 104

april

s	m	t	w	t	f	s
		1	2	3	4	5	6
7	8	9	10	11	12	13
14	15	16	17	18	19	20
21	22	23	24	25	26	27
28	29	30				

Procrastinator Tip

 While working, the brain needs lots of short rests; while not working, the brain doesn't need any rest. Choose wisely.

Things I have to do but that can wait a day, or two, or three . . .

Small things I have to do before I can do the big things I have to do

Things I absolutely have to do unless I absolutely don't want to do them

Things people have been bugging me to do for a really long time

doodle
block

April

monday

15 105

tuesday

16 106

wednesday

17 107

thursday

18 108

GOOD FRIDAY

friday

○ **19** 109

PASSOVER

saturday

20 110

EASTER

sunday

21 111

april

s	m	t	w	t	f	s
	1	2	3	4	5	6
7	8	9	10	11	12	13
14	15	16	17	18	19	20
21	22	23	24	25	26	27
28	29	30				

Procrastinator Activity

 Have you ever looked at the clock five times in two minutes and still had no idea what time it was?

Things I have to do but that can wait a day, or two, or three . . .

Small things I have to do before I can do the big things I have to do

Things I absolutely have to do unless I absolutely don't want to do them

Things people have been bugging me to do for a really long time

doodle
block

April

EARTH DAY *monday*
EASTER MONDAY (CANADA, UK EXCEPT SCOTLAND)

22 112

ST. GEORGE'S DAY (ENGLAND) *tuesday*

23 113

wednesday

24 114

thursday

25 115

friday

◑ **26** 116

saturday

27 117

april

s	m	t	w	t	f	s
		1	2	3	4	5	6
7	8	9	10	11	12	13
14	15	16	17	18	19	20
21	22	23	24	25	26	27
28	29	30				

sunday

28 118

Noble Qualities of Procrastinators

1. We are easily satisfied with our work output.

2. We remain detailed in the face of mounting deadlines.

3. We don't complain about being overlooked to lead new projects.

4. We relish the journey and don't live solely for the results.

5. We obsess over minute details that might matter to, well, someone, someday.

6. We are sentimentalists who savor the success of a task before moving on to another.

7. We are archivists who spend valuable time organizing artifacts, knickknacks, and unfinished work.

8. We never lack for something to do.

List the 10 best years of your life so far. Then figure out what made them so and do more of that.

1. _____

2. _____

3. _____

4. _____

5. _____

6. _____

7. _____

8. _____

9. _____

10. _____

Procrastinator Tip

 A day planner is a place to plan your day. *What* you plan is where the creativity comes in.

Things I have to do but that can wait a day, or two, or three . . .

Small things I have to do before I can do the big things I have to do

Things I absolutely have to do unless I absolutely don't want to do them

Things people have been bugging me to do for a really long time

doodle
block

monday

29 119

tuesday

30 120

wednesday

1 121

thursday

2 122

friday

3 123

saturday

● **4** 124

may						
s	*m*	*t*	*w*	*t*	*f*	*s*
				1	2	3	4
5	6	7	8	9	10	11
12	13	14	15	16	17	18
19	20	21	22	23	24	25
26	27	28	29	30	31	

CINCO DE MAYO

sunday

5 125

Procrastinator Wisdom

When you open your mind, the possibilities in life are endless. It takes a lot of time to ponder them all.

Things I have to do but that can wait a day, or two, or three . . .

Small things I have to do before I can do the big things I have to do

Things I absolutely have to do unless I absolutely don't want to do them

Things people have been bugging me to do for a really long time

doodle
block

May

BANK HOLIDAY (UK)
RAMADAN

monday

6 126

tuesday

7 127

wednesday

8 128

thursday

9 129

friday

10 130

saturday

11 131

MOTHER'S DAY

sunday

 12 132

Procrastinator Tip

If you're going to have a to-do list, it's only fair that you have a to-delay list.

Things I have to do but that can wait a day, or two, or three . . .

Small things I have to do before I can do the big things I have to do

Things I absolutely have to do unless I absolutely don't want to do them

Things people have been bugging me to do for a really long time

doodle
block

May

monday

13 <small>133</small>

tuesday

14 <small>134</small>

wednesday

15 <small>135</small>

thursday

16 <small>136</small>

friday

17 <small>137</small>

ARMED FORCES DAY

saturday

○ **18** <small>138</small>

sunday

19 <small>139</small>

may

s	m	t	w	t	f	s
			1	2	3	4
5	6	7	8	9	10	11
12	13	14	15	16	17	18
19	20	21	22	23	24	25
26	27	28	29	30	31	

Procrastinator Wisdom

 I much prefer having done to having to do.

Things I have to do but that can wait a day, or two, or three . . .

Small things I have to do before I can do the big things I have to do

Things I absolutely have to do unless I absolutely don't want to do them

Things people have been bugging me to do for a really long time

doodle
block

May

VICTORIA DAY (CANADA)

monday

20 140

tuesday

21 141

wednesday

22 142

thursday

23 143

friday

24 144

saturday

25 145

sunday

◑ **26** 146

may

s	m	t	w	t	f	s
			1	2	3	4
5	6	7	8	9	10	11
12	13	14	15	16	17	18
19	20	21	22	23	24	25
26	27	28	29	30	31	

Advanced Procrastination
Techniques for around the House

1. Visit three home-improvement stores in search of the perfect address plaque.

2. Clean the outside of your outdoor trash cans.

3. Tighten every screw in your house—electrical switch plates, doorjambs, closets, drawers, etc.

4. Clean your lawn sprinkler heads of dirt and debris.

5. Test every battery in your home with a battery tester, then make purchasing decisions for the coming year.

6. Clean out the cobwebs from beneath your porch and back deck.

7. Start a light bulb longevity chart to compare the usage in each room.

8. Check the levels of your toiletries and cleaning supplies in the hopes that you'll have to make a trip to the store.

9. Clean the inside and outside of your mailbox.

10. Research and label each tree and plant on your property.

List your 10 favorite
or least favorite aromas.

1. _____

2. _____

3. _____

4. _____

5. _____

6. _____

7. _____

8. _____

9. _____

10. _____

Procrastinator Activity

 Plan for tomorrow, procrastinate today!

Things I have to do but that can wait a day, or two, or three . . .

Small things I have to do before I can do the big things I have to do

Things I absolutely have to do unless I absolutely don't want to do them

Things people have been bugging me to do for a really long time

doodle block

May/Jun

MEMORIAL DAY
BANK HOLIDAY (UK)

monday

27 147

tuesday

28 148

wednesday

29 149

thursday

30 150

friday

31 151

saturday

1 152

sunday

2 153

Procrastinator Tip

Intent is as valuable as action. Don't undervalue it or rush past it!

Things I have to do but that can wait a day, or two, or three . . .

Small things I have to do before I can do the big things I have to do

Things I absolutely have to do unless I absolutely don't want to do them

Things people have been bugging me to do for a really long time

June

---

monday

● **3** 154

EID AL-FITR · *tuesday*

4 155

---

wednesday

5 156

---

thursday

6 157

---

friday

7 158

---

saturday

8 159

---

sunday

9 160

june

s	m	t	w	t	f	s
						1
2	3	4	5	6	7	8
9	10	11	12	13	14	15
16	17	18	19	20	21	22
23	24	25	26	27	28	29
30						

Procrastinator Wisdom

If people have been working for all these years, shouldn't everything be done by now?

Things I have to do but that can wait a day, or two, or three . . .

Small things I have to do before I can do the big things I have to do

Things I absolutely have to do unless I absolutely don't want to do them

Things people have been bugging me to do for a really long time

doodle
block

June

monday

◐ **10** 161

tuesday

11 162

wednesday

12 163

thursday

13 164

FLAG DAY

friday

14 165

saturday

15 166

FATHER'S DAY

sunday

16 167

june

s	m	t	w	t	f	s
						1
2	3	4	5	6	7	8
9	10	11	12	13	14	15
16	17	18	19	20	21	22
23	24	25	26	27	28	29
30						

Procrastinator Tip

Research shows that there's a 50% chance that an undesirable task will disappear if left alone for 30 days.

Things I have to do but that can wait a day, or two, or three . . .

Small things I have to do before I can do the big things I have to do

Things I absolutely have to do unless I absolutely don't want to do them

Things people have been bugging me to do for a really long time

doodle
block

June

monday

○ **17** 168

tuesday

18 169

wednesday

19 170

thursday

20 171

SUMMER SOLSTICE 15:54 UTC

friday

21 172

saturday

22 173

sunday

23 174

june

s	m	t	w	t	f	s
						1
2	3	4	5	6	7	8
9	10	11	12	13	14	15
16	17	18	19	20	21	22
23	24	25	26	27	28	29
30						

Procrastinator Wisdom

They say work makes the time go more quickly. No thanks. I prefer my time to be slow and pleasurable.

Things I have to do but that can wait a day, or two, or three . . .

Small things I have to do before I can do the big things I have to do

Things I absolutely have to do unless I absolutely don't want to do them

Things people have been bugging me to do for a really long time

doodle
block

June

monday
24 175

tuesday
◐ **25** 176

wednesday
26 177

thursday
27 178

friday
28 179

saturday
29 180

sunday
30 181

june

s	m	t	w	t	f	s
						1
2	3	4	5	6	7	8
9	10	11	12	13	14	15
16	17	18	19	20	21	22
23	24	25	26	27	28	29
30						

10 Things to Say to Annoy an Uptight Perfectionist

1. "I'll get around to it soon."

2. "That looks about right."

3. "Take it easy."

4. "Life's too short."

5. "Well, we'll just see what happens."

6. "You never know."

7. "Somehow it'll all work out in the end."

8. "It's out of our hands now."

9. "Don't worry, be happy."

10. "It is what it is."

List 10 home-improvement projects you've never done before, and imagine yourself doing them.

1. _____

2. _____

3. _____

4. _____

5. _____

6. _____

7. _____

8. _____

9. _____

10. _____

Procrastinator Activity

Don't sweat the small stuff—
just don't do any of it.

Things I have to do but that can wait a day, or two, or three . . .

Small things I have to do before I can do the big things I have to do

Things I absolutely have to do unless I absolutely don't want to do them

Things people have been bugging me to do for a really long time

July

CANADA DAY (CANADA)

monday

1 182

tuesday

● **2** 183

wednesday

3 184

INDEPENDENCE DAY

thursday

4 185

friday

5 186

saturday

6 187

sunday

7 188

july

s	m	t	w	t	f	s
	1	2	3	4	5	6
7	8	9	10	11	12	13
14	15	16	17	18	19	20
21	22	23	24	25	26	27
28	29	30	31			

Procrastinator Tip

If time is money, it would seem that procrastinating would be the best way to spend it.

Things I have to do but that can wait a day, or two, or three . . .

Small things I have to do before I can do the big things I have to do

Things I absolutely have to do unless I absolutely don't want to do them

Things people have been bugging me to do for a really long time

doodle
block

July

---

monday

8 189

---

tuesday

◑ **9** 190

---

wednesday

10 191

---

thursday

11 192

BATTLE OF THE BOYNE (N. IRELAND)   *friday*

12 193

---

saturday

13 194

---

sunday

14 195

july

s	m	t	w	t	f	s
	1	2	3	4	5	6
7	8	9	10	11	12	13
14	15	16	17	18	19	20
21	22	23	24	25	26	27
28	29	30	31			

Procrastinator Wisdom

There's enough literature on curing procrastination; it's time for a new emphasis on how best to enjoy it.

Things I have to do but that can wait a day, or two, or three . . .

Small things I have to do before I can do the big things I have to do

Things I absolutely have to do unless I absolutely don't want to do them

Things people have been bugging me to do for a really long time

July

monday

15 196

tuesday

○ **16** 197

wednesday

17 198

thursday

18 199

friday

19 200

saturday

20 201

sunday

21 202

july

s	m	t	w	t	f	s
		1	2	3	4	5	6
7	8	9	10	11	12	13
14	15	16	17	18	19	20
21	22	23	24	25	26	27
28	29	30	31			

Procrastinator Tip

When faced with an endless to-do list, remember: a pencil can erase, a pen can cross off, paper can be recycled or thrown away, and computer files can be deleted.

Things I have to do but that can wait a day, or two, or three . . .

Small things I have to do before I can do the big things I have to do

Things I absolutely have to do unless I absolutely don't want to do them

Things people have been bugging me to do for a really long time

doodle
block

July

monday
22 ₂₀₃

tuesday
23 ₂₀₄

wednesday
24 ₂₀₅

thursday
◐ **25** ₂₀₆

friday
26 ₂₀₇

saturday
27 ₂₀₈

sunday
28 ₂₀₉

july

s	m	t	w	t	f	s
		1	2	3	4	5	6
7	8	9	10	11	12	13
14	15	16	17	18	19	20
21	22	23	24	25	26	27
28	29	30	31			

The World Needs More Conservationists

1. Preserve space on your to-do list for unexpected, frivolous activities.

2. Work in a slow, thoughtful manner to conserve energy.

3. Never leave work so late that you need to use your car headlights.

4. Use telepathy in place of printed documents.

5. Make your office furniture multipurpose. A desk makes a fine footrest, but it can also be used occasionally as a work surface.

6. Shut down your computer for fifteen minutes each hour. The benefits are multitudinous and obvious.

7. Well-digested food converts more easily to energy. Chew slowly.

8. Rest your mind by chanting "om" or anything else that works for you, like "not now" or "time is on my side."

Connect with 10 insects and give each one a name, like Archie the Aphid or Farley the Fly.

1. _____

2. _____

3. _____

4. _____

5. _____

6. _____

7. _____

8. _____

9. _____

10. _____

Procrastinator Activity

In the face of a flood of work, build a raft and float downstream.

Things I have to do but that can wait a day, or two, or three . . .

Small things I have to do before I can do the big things I have to do

Things I absolutely have to do unless I absolutely don't want to do them

Things people have been bugging me to do for a really long time

doodle
block

Jul / Aug

monday

29 210

tuesday

30 211

wednesday

31 212

thursday

● **1** 213

friday

2 214

saturday

3 215

sunday

4 216

august

s	m	t	w	t	f	s
				1	2	3
4	5	6	7	8	9	10
11	12	13	14	15	16	17
18	19	20	21	22	23	24
25	26	27	28	29	30	31

Procrastinator Wisdom

Work may be the fruit of your labor, but procrastination is the spice of life.

Things I have to do but that can wait a day, or two, or three . . .

Small things I have to do before I can do the big things I have to do

Things I absolutely have to do unless I absolutely don't want to do them

Things people have been bugging me to do for a really long time

doodle
block ⌐

August

CIVIC HOLIDAY (CANADA, MOST PROVINCES) *monday*
BANK HOLIDAY (SCOTLAND)

5 217

tuesday

6 218

wednesday

◑ **7** 219

thursday

8 220

friday

9 221

saturday

10 222

august						
s	*m*	*t*	*w*	*t*	*f*	*s*
				1	2	3
4	5	6	7	8	9	10
11	12	13	14	15	16	17
18	19	20	21	22	23	24
25	26	27	28	29	30	31

EID AL-ADHA *sunday*

11 223

Procrastinator Tip

If you don't procrastinate every now and then, how will you appreciate work?

Things I have to do but that can wait a day, or two, or three . . .

Small things I have to do before I can do the big things I have to do

Things I absolutely have to do unless I absolutely don't want to do them

Things people have been bugging me to do for a really long time

August

doodle
block

monday

12 224

tuesday

13 225

wednesday

14 226

thursday

○ **15** 227

friday

16 228

saturday

17 229

sunday

18 230

august

s	m	t	w	t	f	s
				1	2	3
4	5	6	7	8	9	10
11	12	13	14	15	16	17
18	19	20	21	22	23	24
25	26	27	28	29	30	31

Procrastinator Activity

A garden is a beautiful excuse to shut out the world and do little else.

Things I have to do but that can wait a day, or two, or three . . .

Small things I have to do before I can do the big things I have to do

Things I absolutely have to do unless I absolutely don't want to do them

Things people have been bugging me to do for a really long time

August

monday

19 231

tuesday

20 232

wednesday

21 233

thursday

22 234

friday

◑ **23** 235

saturday

24 236

sunday

25 237

august

s	m	t	w	t	f	s
				1	2	3
4	5	6	7	8	9	10
11	12	13	14	15	16	17
18	19	20	21	22	23	24
25	26	27	28	29	30	31

Must-Haves for Any Procrastinator's Office

1. A large computer monitor to block the view of coworkers passing by.

2. A chair that reclines to a comfortable sleeping position.

3. A Ganesha statue to remove obstacles and act as a conversation piece.

4. A rubber-band ball in progress.

5. A small foldaway cot for afternoon siestas.

6. A dart board for posting old to-do lists.

7. A miniature golf course on your desk using marbles for golf balls and pencil cups for each hole.

8. A chart of chair exercises.

9. An exercise ball. For bouncing, of course.

Create 10 different superheroes who have the power to solve all the world's problems.

1. _____

2. _____

3. _____

4. _____

5. _____

6. _____

7. _____

8. _____

9. _____

10. _____

Procrastinator Wisdom

 In a society that tweets about every nanosecond of life, doing nothing is something to crow about!

Things I have to do but that can wait a day, or two, or three . . .

Small things I have to do before I can do the big things I have to do

Things I absolutely have to do unless I absolutely don't want to do them

Things people have been bugging me to do for a really long time

doodle
block

BANK HOLIDAY (UK EXCEPT SCOTLAND)   *monday*

26 238

tuesday

27 239

wednesday

28 240

thursday

29 241

friday

● **30** 242

MUHARRAM   *saturday*

31 243

sunday

1 244

september

s	m	t	w	t	f	s
	1	2	3	4	5	6	7
8	9	10	11	12	13	14
15	16	17	18	19	20	21
22	23	24	25	26	27	28
29	30					

Procrastinator Tip

If you look twice before you cross the street, why wouldn't you think twice before you tackle a difficult task?

Things I have to do but that can wait a day, or two, or three . . .

Small things I have to do before I can do the big things I have to do

Things I absolutely have to do unless I absolutely don't want to do them

Things people have been bugging me to do for a really long time

doodle block

September

LABOR DAY

monday

2 245

tuesday

3 246

wednesday

4 247

thursday

5 248

friday

◐ 6 249

saturday

7 250

sunday

8 251

Procrastinator Wisdom

In an overstimulated society, procrastination is a savior not a sin.

Things I have to do but that can wait a day, or two, or three . . .

Small things I have to do before I can do the big things I have to do

Things I absolutely have to do unless I absolutely don't want to do them

Things people have been bugging me to do for a really long time

doodle block

September

ASHURA

monday

9 252

tuesday

10 253

wednesday

11 254

thursday

12 255

friday

13 256

saturday

○ **14** 257

sunday

15 258

september

s	m	t	w	t	f	s
	1	2	3	4	5	6	7
8	9	10	11	12	13	14
15	16	17	18	19	20	21
22	23	24	25	26	27	28
29	30					

Procrastinator Activity

 Be a team player: ask everyone in your office what they had for dinner last night and how their evening was before you begin working.

Things I have to do but that can wait a day, or two, or three . . .

Small things I have to do before I can do the big things I have to do

Things I absolutely have to do unless I absolutely don't want to do them

Things people have been bugging me to do for a really long time

doodle
block

September

monday

16 259

tuesday

17 260

wednesday

18 261

thursday

19 262

friday

20 263

INTERNATIONAL DAY OF PEACE

saturday

21 264

sunday

◗ **22** 265

september

s	m	t	w	t	f	s
1	2	3	4	5	6	7
8	9	10	11	12	13	14
15	16	17	18	19	20	21
22	23	24	25	26	27	28
29	30					

Procrastinator Tip

If life is what happens to you while you're busy making other plans, why make any?

Things I have to do but that can wait a day, or two, or three . . .

Small things I have to do before I can do the big things I have to do

Things I absolutely have to do unless I absolutely don't want to do them

Things people have been bugging me to do for a really long time

doodle
block

September

AUTUMNAL EQUINOX 07:50 UTC

monday

23 266

tuesday

24 267

wednesday

25 268

thursday

26 269

friday

27 270

saturday

● **28** 271

sunday

29 272

september

s	m	t	w	t	f	s
1	2	3	4	5	6	7
8	9	10	11	12	13	14
15	16	17	18	19	20	21
22	23	24	25	26	27	28
29	30					

How to Make Killer Art
out of Office Supplies

1. Line up colored pencils of different lengths to make a cool domino maze.

2. Connect paper clips with rubber bands to make a funky necklace or a cheap Christmas tree ornament.

3. Make a group of paper airplanes and turn a document divider upside down for a hanger.

4. Turn file folders upside down to make a teepee village.

5. Make an avant-garde sculpture out of used toner cartridges.

6. Empty your drawer organizer, fill it with sand, and turn it into a Zen garden.

7. Use a pencil cup to plant a bonsai tree.

8. Arrange large reams of paper to make a huge tic-tac-toe board. Use a DVD for O's and two pens crossed for X's.

9. Spell out a "word of the day" on your desk using staples. Make it a really long word.

List 10 super-annoying sounds
that you never want to hear again.

1. _____

2. _____

3. _____

4. _____

5. _____

6. _____

7. _____

8. _____

9. _____

10. _____

Procrastinator Wisdom

 Some people say *nothing* is the worst thing you can do. I challenge them to tell me the last time a war broke out over *nothing*.

Things I have to do but that can wait a day, or two, or three . . .

Small things I have to do before I can do the big things I have to do

Things I absolutely have to do unless I absolutely don't want to do them

Things people have been bugging me to do for a really long time

doodle block

ROSH HASHANAH

monday

30 273

tuesday

1 274

wednesday

2 275

thursday

3 276

friday

4 277

saturday

◑ **5** 278

sunday

6 279

october

s	m	t	w	t	f	s
			1	2	3	4	5
6	7	8	9	10	11	12
13	14	15	16	17	18	19
20	21	22	23	24	25	26
27	28	29	30	31		

Procrastinator Tip

Learning to be productive is about as *exciting* as learning to like kale-based cookies.

Things I have to do but that can wait a day, or two, or three . . .

Small things I have to do before I can do the big things I have to do

Things I absolutely have to do unless I absolutely don't want to do them

Things people have been bugging me to do for a really long time

doodle block

October

monday

7 280

tuesday

8 281

YOM KIPPUR   *wednesday*

9 282

thursday

10 283

friday

11 284

saturday

12 285

sunday

○ **13** 286

october

s	m	t	w	t	f	s
		1	2	3	4	5
6	7	8	9	10	11	12
13	14	15	16	17	18	19
20	21	22	23	24	25	26
27	28	29	30	31		

Procrastinator Wisdom

Procrastination may be a sign of weakness, but it's also a sign of independence and creativity.

Things I have to do but that can wait a day, or two, or three . . .

Small things I have to do before I can do the big things I have to do

Things I absolutely have to do unless I absolutely don't want to do them

Things people have been bugging me to do for a really long time

doodle
block

October

COLUMBUS DAY
THANKSGIVING DAY (CANADA)

monday

14 287

tuesday

15 288

wednesday

16 289

thursday

17 290

friday

18 291

saturday

19 292

sunday

20 293

october

s	m	t	w	t	f	s
		1	2	3	4	5
6	7	8	9	10	11	12
13	14	15	16	17	18	19
20	21	22	23	24	25	26
27	28	29	30	31		

Procrastinator Activity

The art of doing nothing is an art. Respect and cultivate it whenever you can.

Things I have to do but that can wait a day, or two, or three . . .

Small things I have to do before I can do the big things I have to do

Things I absolutely have to do unless I absolutely don't want to do them

Things people have been bugging me to do for a really long time

October

monday

◐ **21** ₂₉₄

tuesday

22 ₂₉₅

wednesday

23 ₂₉₆

UNITED NATIONS DAY

thursday

24 ₂₉₇

friday

25 ₂₉₈

saturday

26 ₂₉₉

october

s	m	t	w	t	f	s
		1	2	3	4	5
6	7	8	9	10	11	12
13	14	15	16	17	18	19
20	21	22	23	24	25	26
27	28	29	30	31		

DIWALI

SUMMER TIME ENDS (UK)

sunday

27 ₃₀₀

Ways to Instantly De-stress

1. Google *people smiling*, then print out your favorite ten photographs and post them on your wall.

2. Gently flow through the halls of your office in a hypnotic tai chi movement.

3. Quickly replace every stress-filled thought with one of joy. The mind can only hold one thought at a time and hopefully it chooses the sunnier one.

4. Spin furiously in your work chair while chanting: *Peace be with me.*

5. Google the life expectancy for someone your age. Then figure out how many minutes you might have left to live—subtracting eight hours each day for sleep. Realize what a waste of precious time stress is!

6. Bust out your air guitar and crank AC-DC.

7. Imagine your work is completed, then choreograph a victory dance and design a creative headdress to wear.

8. Learn how to say *vacation* in thirty different languages.

9. Search online for hotels with the coolest swim-up bars.

Name 10 new ailments that prevent you from doing anything beyond binge-watching. (Like the *schnizzles*: excessive sniffling in times of stress.)

1. _____

2. _____

3. _____

4. _____

5. _____

6. _____

7. _____

8. _____

9. _____

10. _____

Procrastinator Tip

 Procrastination may be bad for you, but isn't everything?

Things I have to do but that can wait a day, or two, or three . . .

Small things I have to do before I can do the big things I have to do

Things I absolutely have to do unless I absolutely don't want to do them

Things people have been bugging me to do for a really long time

doodle
block

monday

● **28** 301

tuesday

29 302

wednesday

30 303

HALLOWEEN

thursday

31 304

friday

1 305

saturday

2 306

DAYLIGHT SAVING TIME ENDS

sunday

3 307

november

s	m	t	w	t	f	s
					1	2
3	4	5	6	7	8	9
10	11	12	13	14	15	16
17	18	19	20	21	22	23
24	25	26	27	28	29	30

Procrastinator Wisdom

 Articles condemning procrastination are written by overworked people who are jealous of procrastinators.

Things I have to do but that can wait a day, or two, or three . . .

Small things I have to do before I can do the big things I have to do

Things I absolutely have to do unless I absolutely don't want to do them

Things people have been bugging me to do for a really long time

doodle
block

November

monday

◑ 4 308

tuesday

5 309

wednesday

6 310

thursday

7 311

friday

8 312

MAWLID AN-NABI

saturday

9 313

REMEMBRANCE DAY (UK)

sunday

10 314

november

s	m	t	w	t	f	s
					1	2
3	4	5	6	7	8	9
10	11	12	13	14	15	16
17	18	19	20	21	22	23
24	25	26	27	28	29	30

Procrastinator Tip

I'd like to find a financial planner who can help me invest in my future while I procrastinate in the present.

Things I have to do but that can wait a day, or two, or three . . .

Small things I have to do before I can do the big things I have to do

Things I absolutely have to do unless I absolutely don't want to do them

Things people have been bugging me to do for a really long time

doodle block

November

VETERANS DAY
REMEMBRANCE DAY (CANADA)

monday

11 315

tuesday

○ 12 316

wednesday

13 317

thursday

14 318

friday

15 319

saturday

16 320

sunday

17 321

november

s	m	t	w	t	f	s
					1	2
3	4	5	6	7	8	9
10	11	12	13	14	15	16
17	18	19	20	21	22	23
24	25	26	27	28	29	30

Procrastinator Activity

Every day you have three choices: work on nothing, work on something less important, or work on something more important. Choose wisely.

Things I have to do but that can wait a day, or two, or three . . .

Small things I have to do before I can do the big things I have to do

Things I absolutely have to do unless I absolutely don't want to do them

Things people have been bugging me to do for a really long time

doodle
block

November

monday

18 322

tuesday

◑ **19** 323

wednesday

20 324

thursday

21 325

friday

22 326

saturday

23 327

sunday

24 328

Now or Later, You Decide

1. Now is rigid, later is flexible.

2. Now is defined, later is mysterious.

3. Now is obvious, later is surprising.

4. Now is stressful, later is soothing.

5. Now is done, later is becoming.

6. Now is hurried, later is thoughtful.

7. Now is needy, later is generous.

8. Now is commitment, later is promise.

9. Now is final, later is new beginnings.

List 10 things you miss from your childhood. Be sure to include your favorite candy!

1. _____

2. _____

3. _____

4. _____

5. _____

6. _____

7. _____

8. _____

9. _____

10. _____

Procrastinator Wisdom

At the end of the day, the way I look at work is: if it didn't happen, it wasn't meant to be.

Things I have to do but that can wait a day, or two, or three . . .

Small things I have to do before I can do the big things I have to do

Things I absolutely have to do unless I absolutely don't want to do them

Things people have been bugging me to do for a really long time

doodle
block

monday

25 ₃₂₉

tuesday

● **26** ₃₃₀

wednesday

27 ₃₃₁

THANKSGIVING DAY   *thursday*

28 ₃₃₂

friday

29 ₃₃₃

ST. ANDREW'S DAY (SCOTLAND)   *saturday*

30 ₃₃₄

december

s	m	t	w	t	f	s
	1	2	3	4	5	6	7
8	9	10	11	12	13	14
15	16	17	18	19	20	21
22	23	24	25	26	27	28
29	30	31				

sunday

1 ₃₃₅

Procrastinator Tip

Life expectancy has increased greatly. Procrastination is an excellent way to insure that you'll have things to do your entire life.

Things I have to do but that can wait a day, or two, or three . . .

Small things I have to do before I can do the big things I have to do

Things I absolutely have to do unless I absolutely don't want to do them

Things people have been bugging me to do for a really long time

doodle
block

December

monday

2 ₃₃₆

---

tuesday

3 ₃₃₇

---

wednesday

◑ **4** ₃₃₈

---

thursday

5 ₃₃₉

---

friday

6 ₃₄₀

---

saturday

7 ₃₄₁

---

december

s	m	t	w	t	f	s
1	2	3	4	5	6	7
8	9	10	11	12	13	14
15	16	17	18	19	20	21
22	23	24	25	26	27	28
29	30	31				

sunday

8 ₃₄₂

Procrastinator Wisdom

Procrastinators avoid one thing by doing another; it's much more productive than doing nothing!

Things I have to do but that can wait a day, or two, or three . . .

Small things I have to do before I can do the big things I have to do

Things I absolutely have to do unless I absolutely don't want to do them

Things people have been bugging me to do for a really long time

doodle
block

December

monday

9 343

tuesday

10 344

wednesday

11 345

thursday

○ **12** 346

friday

13 347

saturday

14 348

sunday

15 349

december

s	m	t	w	t	f	s
	1	2	3	4	5	6	7
8	9	10	11	12	13	14
15	16	17	18	19	20	21
22	23	24	25	26	27	28
29	30	31				

Procrastinator Tip

 Overcoming procrastination is like overcoming ice cream. You can do it, but you'll regret it.

Things I have to do but that can wait a day, or two, or three . . .

Small things I have to do before I can do the big things I have to do

Things I absolutely have to do unless I absolutely don't want to do them

Things people have been bugging me to do for a really long time

December

monday

16 350

tuesday

17 351

wednesday

18 352

thursday

◑ **19** 353

friday

20 354

saturday

21 355

december

s	m	t	w	t	f	s
	1	2	3	4	5	6	7
8	9	10	11	12	13	14
15	16	17	18	19	20	21
22	23	24	25	26	27	28
29	30	31				

WINTER SOLSTICE 04:19 UTC

sunday

22 356

Procrastinator Activity

 Alphabetize your herbs and spices. Then research the culinary history of each.

Things I have to do but that can wait a day, or two, or three . . .

Small things I have to do before I can do the big things I have to do

Things I absolutely have to do unless I absolutely don't want to do them

Things people have been bugging me to do for a really long time

doodle block

December

HANUKKAH

monday

23 357

tuesday

24 358

CHRISTMAS

wednesday

25 359

BOXING DAY (CANADA, UK)
KWANZAA BEGINS

thursday

● **26** 360

friday

27 361

saturday

28 362

sunday

29 363

december

s	m	t	w	t	f	s
1	2	3	4	5	6	7
8	9	10	11	12	13	14
15	16	17	18	19	20	21
22	23	24	25	26	27	28
29	30	31				

Procrastinator Tip

When you've fallen behind, the only way to catch up is to cross difficult tasks off your to-do list.

Things I have to do but that can wait a day, or two, or three . . .

Small things I have to do before I can do the big things I have to do

Things I absolutely have to do unless I absolutely don't want to do them

Things people have been bugging me to do for a really long time

doodle block

monday

30 364

tuesday

31 365

NEW YEAR'S DAY   *wednesday*

1 1

BANK HOLIDAY (SCOTLAND)   *thursday*

2 2

friday

◑ **3** 3

saturday

4 4

sunday

5 5

january

s	m	t	w	t	f	s
				1	2	3	4
5	6	7	8	9	10	11
12	13	14	15	16	17	18
19	20	21	22	23	24	25
26	27	28	29	30	31	

Grace Periods for Bills Due & Tax Extension Schedule/Plan

1. _____

2. _____

3. _____

4. _____

5. _____

6. _____

7. _____

8. _____

9. _____

10. _____

People to Call or Text
When You Don't Feel Like Working

NAME   MOBILE

                        PHONE (H)

                        PHONE (W)

NAME   MOBILE

                        PHONE (H)

                        PHONE (W)

NAME   MOBILE

                        PHONE (H)

                        PHONE (W)

NAME   MOBILE

                        PHONE (H)

                        PHONE (W)

january

s	m	t	w	t	f	s
			1	2	3	4
5	6	7	8	9	10	11
12	13	14	15	16	17	18
19	20	21	22	23	24	25
26	27	28	29	30	31	

february

s	m	t	w	t	f	s
						1
2	3	4	5	6	7	8
9	10	11	12	13	14	15
16	17	18	19	20	21	22
23	24	25	26	27	28	29

march

s	m	t	w	t	f	s
1	2	3	4	5	6	7
8	9	10	11	12	13	14
15	16	17	18	19	20	21
22	23	24	25	26	27	28
29	30	31				

april

s	m	t	w	t	f	s
			1	2	3	4
5	6	7	8	9	10	11
12	13	14	15	16	17	18
19	20	21	22	23	24	25
26	27	28	29	30		

may

s	m	t	w	t	f	s
					1	2
3	4	5	6	7	8	9
10	11	12	13	14	15	16
17	18	19	20	21	22	23
24	25	26	27	28	29	30
31						

june

s	m	t	w	t	f	s
	1	2	3	4	5	6
7	8	9	10	11	12	13
14	15	16	17	18	19	20
21	22	23	24	25	26	27
28	29	30				

july

s	m	t	w	t	f	s
			1	2	3	4
5	6	7	8	9	10	11
12	13	14	15	16	17	18
19	20	21	22	23	24	25
26	27	28	29	30	31	

august

s	m	t	w	t	f	s
						1
2	3	4	5	6	7	8
9	10	11	12	13	14	15
16	17	18	19	20	21	22
23	24	25	26	27	28	29
30	31					

september

s	m	t	w	t	f	s
		1	2	3	4	5
6	7	8	9	10	11	12
13	14	15	16	17	18	19
20	21	22	23	24	25	26
27	28	29	30			

october

s	m	t	w	t	f	s
				1	2	3
4	5	6	7	8	9	10
11	12	13	14	15	16	17
18	19	20	21	22	23	24
25	26	27	28	29	30	31

november

s	m	t	w	t	f	s
1	2	3	4	5	6	7
8	9	10	11	12	13	14
15	16	17	18	19	20	21
22	23	24	25	26	27	28
29	30					

december

s	m	t	w	t	f	s
		1	2	3	4	5
6	7	8	9	10	11	12
13	14	15	16	17	18	19
20	21	22	23	24	25	26
27	28	29	30	31		